ACKNOWLEDGEMENT

First and foremost I would like to thank almighty god for making me survive the most part of 2020, and during the period of lockdown only I could pen down my thoughts.

By the grace of God I am blessed to have parents who were very supportive throughout the journey of my life. It's because of their dedication, their teachings, their principle is for what I am able to collect my thoughts and pen them.

I am deeply thankful to my sisters and colleagues whom I have disturbed night out to have a read and give recommendations if my poems are worth reading. I know I have troubled them a lot. But it's because of them I am able to pen this book.

THANK YOU ALL.

AMRITESH KUMAR

INTRODUCTION

This book is basically a collection of poems ranging in depths of motivation, fiction and romance.

The motivation section is basically the truth and the harsh realities of life that everyone undergoes. Our will power, our goals, our memories, our journeys and our rationale ideas have been compiled.

The fiction is basically my imagination. I don't know how many authors write 500 or more pages book. I have a story and I love to convert it into a poem.

The romantic portion basically deals with heartbreak and how to get over it :-)

Hope my readers will enjoy my collection :):)

EMPTY ROADS

Let's walk down these empty roads

To breathe fresh air without any odds

Though years have passed

Springs have gone

Brings back my childhood

These empty roads

Shutters of memories

Suddenly rolled by

When I strolled on

These empty roads

Could hear the similar chirp

And rustling of leaves

When I pass by

These empty roads

Tears of joy

Rolled down by my eyes

As the nature whispered

I love these empty roads

WORTH THE WAIT

A perfect sunrise

A perfect sunset

Doesn't come at once

Sometimes it's worth the wait

A delicious coffee

A perfect date

A perfect love

Sometimes it's worth the wait

Tides might be high

The sailor still navigates

To reach the shore

Sometimes it's worth the wait

Life is like a curve

It's not straight

You may turn right or left

Or maybe even pause

Sometimes it's worth the wait

You may fail a million times

Opportunities might come late

Just believe in your hard work

Sometimes it's worth the wait

The wait may be long

You might even hate

Don't you worry my friend

Sometimes it's worth the wait

HAS TO END

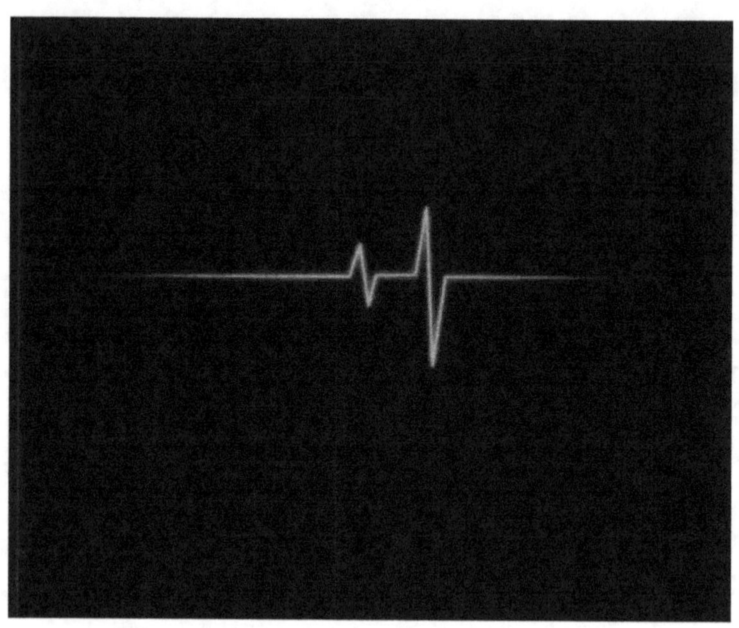

What is born

What is formed

Here in this world

Has to end

What we have learned

What we have achieved

One day

Has to end

What we love

What we cherish

One day

Has to end

What we have or not

Aspirations fulfilled or not

What is material

Has to end

Once child

Then adult

After the old age

Has to end

Live your life

Love your life

As one day

Has to end

ONE DAY

For what is unfathomable

One day

Will be penetrable

For what is spurious

One day

Will be reality

For what is hard

One day

Will be cakewalk

For every dark cloud

There's a silver lining

One day

Your sun will rise

One day

Hard times will fly

One day

You will touch the skies

One day

You will reach so high

The day say good bye

God will cry

Again there'll be a dark cloud

Just open your eyes

SOMETIMES I WISH

Sometimes I wish

I could change the past

Sometimes I wish

I could go back in time

Sometimes I wish

I could amend my wrongs

Sometimes I wish

I could relive the past

But

It's the past

For what I am today

It's the past

For what I have learnt

It's the past

For what I have gained

Past is lost

But memories

Are the ones

Which I cherish the most

WHAT'S LEFT BEHIND

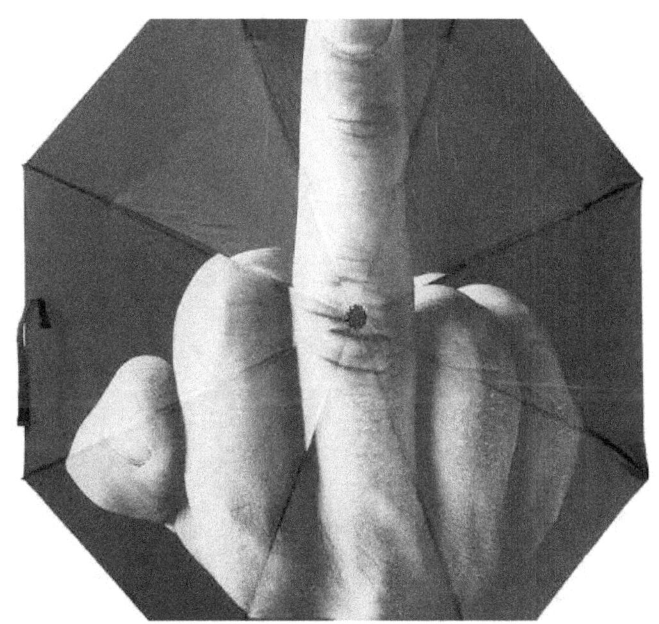

What's left behind

Is we care

What's left behind

Is we fear

What's left behind

Is for what are tears

What's left behind

Should be left

For the things we aspire

Should we endeavor

Enjoy today

Cause for tomorrow

I don't care

SIT ALONE

Occasionally I sit alone

This moment I realize

What's right what's wrong

Occasionally I sit alone

To take decisions

Which makes me strong

Occasionally I sit alone

As to realize

Where do I belong

Occasionally I sit alone

What's the purpose

Of my life all along

But this time I sat

In the midst of rain

Just to hear the nature's song

A WALK

First step

Your parents taught

That was a walk

First day at school

Crying out loud

That was a walk

Sneaking out

Towards playground

That was a walk

Moving out

Establishing yourself

That was a walk

There is a walk

In every walk of life

Walk the odds

For a meaningful and happy life

TAKE ME BACK

Scrolling these days

I wonder

Take me back

Remembering the days

I wonder

Take me back

Sudden burst of emotions

I wonder

Take me back

Inherent good feelings

I wonder

Take me back

The Duchenne smile

I wonder

Take me back

Memories are priceless

I wonder

Let's go back

PERCEPTION

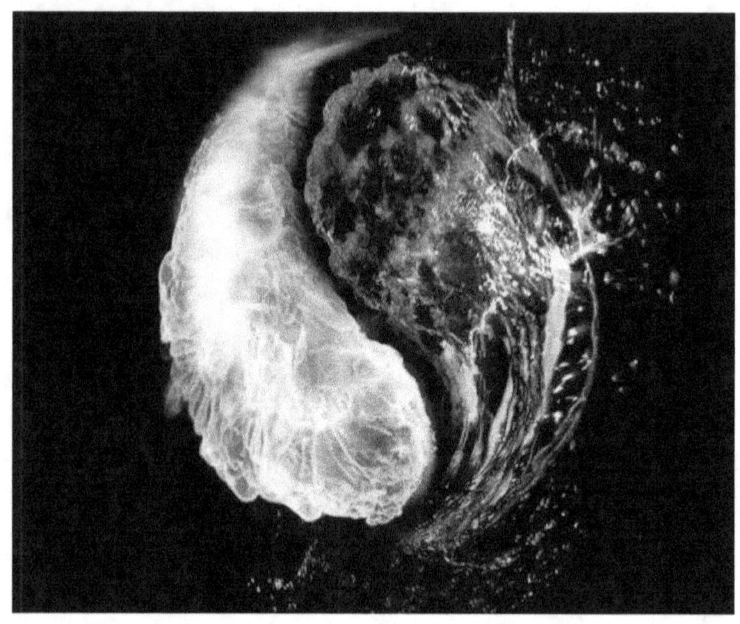

Perception is what

It's all about

Light and dark

Complement each other

For without coal

There is no diamond

Neither yin nor yang

Is absolute

Nothing is difficult

Nothing is easy

For who masters

Art of balancing

Makes difficult ones easy

I DON'T CARE

I don't care

If I eat or sleep

I don't care

If there is day or night

I don't care

For shadow in a tree

I don't care

If I am alright

For I care

Is the well-being of

Men under me

For what I see

If they are happy

The most happiest is inner me

SUNNY DAY

Sunny day was it

Sky was lit

Day was gloomy

Lying in my hole

Trying to set goals

Sweats dripping

Mind distracting a bit

Sunny day was it

Sudden urge to relax myself

Go to a place somewhat cooler

Can't execute it

Sunny day was it

Trying to find a shade

But mankind has made it fade

For the future generations

I was afraid

Numerous thoughts

Mind buzzing like bee

Suddenly someone asked for Tea

Everything was calm

I have to admit

Being Vinci I quit

I was relaxed a bit

Sunny day was it

IF

If you fall

Rise up and shine

Don't look for a hand

Cause they are behind

If you are sad

Put up a smile

Don't look for a face

Cause they are behind

If you fail

Work hard today

You will bloom

Who has seen the next day

Failures, leave it

Success, believe it

Put efforts everyday

Cause Rome was not built in a day

LIFE IS MATHS

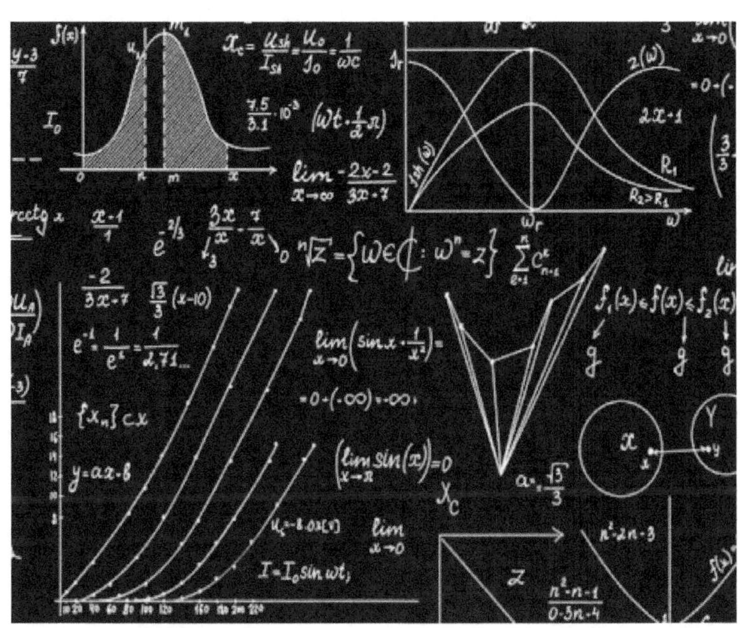

Life is Math

Differentiation you reduce

Integration you prosper

Sometimes

Complex questions

Might have the

Simplest of answer

If alone

You are a point

If together

You set a line

Two parallel lines

Never intersect each other

Similarly radical persons

Never go along together

Life is Math

We add hope

Subtract the sorrows

Multiply the happiness

Divided we fall apart

Probability of success

Is high

If you believe

In your art

MASTERMIND

Mastermind on a roll

Wanted: DEAD or ALIVE

Anyone catches

Will get a Million Five

Everyone eyes

Popped out open wide

For they became vigilant

Throughout night

False claims of catch

They were normal

In the midst of this

Police received a Phone call

Familiar voice

Catch me if you can

Saturday night I will be

Robbing the Federal Bank

Security beefed up

Escape routes blocked

Order by governor

Patrols round the clock

Nothing happened,

Everyone thinking

Was it a Prank?

It's Mastermind, Take no risk

Said the governor

He decided to visit the bank

Managers and others

Jobs were at stake

Pleaded in front of governor

Please help !! For god's sake

Let's move the cash

Somewhere safe

Governor suggested

National treasure chest

Money loaded in the van

Escorts and security lined up

For move towards

The treasure hub

Governor came out

Someone pulled out a gun

Aiming at governor said

Your game is over son

A Police aiming

At governor's head

Shouted the governor

Shoot the mastermind!!

Even though I'm dead

Policeman smirked and

Closer he moved

Pulled out the governor's mask

Shocked everyone stood

Policeman said –

Now I'll have a million five

Mastermind said - Shhhh

And he vanished

Lost was everyone

What just happened?

Mastermind woke up smiling

And said

Come On man:

This was a dream of mine

FLIGHT OF A BIRD

Sky was dark

Rains pouring in

Cracked open the shell

Baby bird felt the mother's skin

Lost innocent eyes

Searching for a face

Eyes met

And it felt her grace

Aah beautiful !! Exclaimed the mother

And a distant voice

Let's train it

Will fetch a good price

Mother's joyous ride

Came to a sudden halt

Eyes became moist

And tears started to roll

She moved closer

And cuddled the baby bird

Whispered in her ears

Outside, There is a beautiful world

Quickly learned

To sing and dance

To see the outside world

This was her only chance

Auction and sold

Amazing! Exclaimed the owner

Let's give surprise

To our lovely little daughter

Baby bird moved outside

Only to be caged

Is this outside world mother?

Was filled with anger and rage

Neither did it eat

Nor did it dance and sing

Day after day just growing weak

"Maybe it's due to cage",

Said the sweet lovely little being

Cage was set open

Emotions were high

Baby bird started to eat, dance

And sing in a beautiful voice

As Days passed

Melodious became the voice

She roamed around the house

Filled with pride

She was lost

In her own beautiful world

Suddenly she felt aghast

When she heard someone sing

A more beautiful chord

Inching closer

Wondering from where it came

She moved towards

The window pane

Not one but many she saw

Utterly shocked

Realizing her beautiful world was

A bigger cage where she was locked

Desperate to go out

Tried every corner

Failed, Didn't give up

And tried more harder

Suddenly it's eyes

Went to a fire place

It climbed up and finally

Felt the space

Saw others flying

It didn't know how?

Jumped down the building

Gravity pulling her down

She tried to dance, tried to sing

Tried to repeat the show

Still going down

Crashed onto a window

Became unconscious

All the beautiful memories

Of mother came crashing too

She tried to touch her mother

But couldn't

Tried even more harder

Finally! She felt her touch

Suddenly her eyes opened

And she was in the skies

The flight of the bird

Was remarkably high

Singing, Dancing and Flying !

She said

Mother you were right throughout

Outside world is beautiful

There is no doubt

STORY OF A TOWN

In the Far East, along the river

There located a Town

Prosperity and happiness

In it was profound

One fine day

Town was attacked

Defeated and broken

It was rampaged

Sorrow and misery

Was common place in Town

Taxes and slavery

Imposed by the crown

Anyone going rogue

Or raising an eye

Would be sent to prison

Or sentenced to die

Jack and Mark

The best of the friends

Decided to bring all this

To an end

Refused by many

Only few stick around

The syndicate only motto

Was to liberate the town

Plunders and loot

Started to happen

The monarch was furious

And decided to take an action

Bounty was set

Shoot at sight

I want everyone's head

By midnight

Fearing of their lives

Someone gave a tip

The syndicate hideout

In a remote strip

Whole army moved

Gheraoed the location

Surrender or die

Were there only option

Nothing moved

Not even a sound

Soldiers realised

Something fishy was around

They charged the camp

Broke inside

Only to find royal guards

With their mouths taped tight

Panicky struck

Everyone rushed towards the palace

Shocked to see Jack and Mark

With guns pointed at Monarch's face

Drop your guns

Or they will shoot

Monarch said, "Do it at once"

Without a doubt

Orders are orders

Dropped the guns

Came from behind

The local ones

They picked the guns

Fired in skies

As the monarchy was told

To leave their town,

And say good bye

Agreed the monarch

Asked for horses

They left barefoot

As request denied by the audience

Wait said Mark

I have something to offer you mate

Turned back Monarch

Smilingly said Mark

Only donkeys in your fate

Fumed was the monarch

Couldn't do a thing

Left the town

And the town was back

To its original being

CROSSES BY

World full of lies

Without you it's a cage

Everyday this thought crosses by

A Day without you

How can I lose you

This thought crosses by

Sitting in the backyard

Looking at the sky

Memories crosses by

Walking in the lane

Lost I am

Can't believe you left me why

Am alone without you

Left with tears

All I just do is cry

Still am hopeful

Someday you will pass by

To be again with you

Everyday this thought crosses by

THE DAY YOU LEFT

The Day you left

Is the day I cried

For I looked in mirror

Could only see lies

The Day you left

Had myself locked

For only you were

The key to my heart

The Day you left

I went blind

For only you brought

The colours to my eyes

The Day you left

I seemed lost

For only you lead

The direction to my soul

The Day you left

I started to frown

For only you were

The reason for my smile

The Day you left

Day felt like night

For only of you

My life was bright

The Day you left

Felt like

Worst day of my life

Didn't sleep the whole night

Sun-kissed I was

No tears left in my eyes

Went to the mirror

My reflection smiled

And said to me

This is not the end of life

WHEREVER YOU ARE

Didn't change the sheets

Since you have gone

Cause your fragrance in it

Is still on

Was taking a walk

And emotions were high

Cause I was alone

Under the gloomy sky

Went to a club

Music was loud

I felt lost

Within my own crowd

Ordered the same

For you and me again

Cheers I said to our good times

And I drank alone straight

Ordered again

And I was high

There was anger for you

In my eyes

The heart skipped a bit

Sober I was

I just hoped

Stay happy

Wherever you are